上班这件事

Office Workers

李溪 编译

外文出版社

图书在版编目（CIP）数据

上班这件事/李湲编译. —北京：外文出版社，2005（笑话集锦）
ISBN 7-119-04248-3

Ⅰ. 上... Ⅱ. 李... Ⅲ. 英语-对照读物，笑话-英、汉
Ⅳ. H319.4：Ⅰ

中国版本图书馆 CIP 数据核字（2005）第 111268 号

外文出版社网址：
　http://www.flp.com.cn
外文出版社电子信箱：
　info@flp.com.cn
　sales@flp.com.cn

笑话集锦
上班这件事

编　　译　李　湲
责任编辑　李春英
封面设计　李迎迎
印刷监制　冯　浩
出版发行　外文出版社
社　　址　北京市百万庄大街 24 号　　邮政编码　100037
电　　话　(010) 68995883（编辑部）
　　　　　(010) 68329514/68327211（推广发行部）
印　　刷　三河市汇鑫印务有限公司
经　　销　新华书店/外文书店
开　　本　32 开　　　　　　　字　　数　30 千字
印　　数　5001－10000 册　　印　　张　6
版　　次　2006 年第 1 版第 2 次印刷
装　　别　平
书　　号　ISBN 7-119-04248-3
定　　价　9.80 元

Contents

3

In Prison vs. at Work

IN PRISON ... You spend the majority of your time in an 8 × 10 cell.

AT WORK ... You spend most of your time in a 6 × 8 cubicle.

IN PRISON ... You get three meals a day.

AT WORK ... You only get a break for one meal and you have to pay for it.

IN PRISON ... You get time off for good behavior.

AT WORK ... You get rewarded for good behavior with more work.

2

蹲监狱和上班

在监狱里……你大部分时间待在 8×10 大小的牢房里。

上班时……你大部分时间待在 6×8 大小的格子间里。

在监狱里……你一天吃三顿饭。

上班时……你只有一次工间休用来吃饭，而且这顿饭是要付钱的。

在监狱里……你表现好的话会获得减刑。

上班时……对你表现好的奖赏就是更多的工作。

IN PRISON ... A guard locks and unlocks all the doors for you.

AT WORK ... You must carry around a security card and unlock and open all the doors yourself.

IN PRISON ... You can watch TV and play games.

AT WORK ... You get fired for watching TV and playing games.

IN PRISON ... You get your own toilet.

AT WORK ... You have to share.

IN PRISON ... They allow your family and friends to visit.

AT WORK ... You cannot even speak to your family and friends.

在监狱里……有看守为你开关所有的门。

上班时……你得随身带着门禁卡自己动手开所有的门。

在监狱里……你可以看电视和玩儿游戏。

上班时……如果你看电视和玩儿游戏就会被解雇。

在监狱里……你有自己的马桶。

上班时……你得和别人共用马桶。

在监狱里……你的家人和朋友们可以来探视你。

上班时……你甚至都不能和家人和朋友们通话。

上班这件事

IN PRISON ... All expenses are paid by taxpayers with no work required.

AT WORK ... You get to pay all the expenses to go to work and then they deduct taxes from your salary to pay for prisoners.

IN PRISON ... You spend most of your time looking through bars from the inside wanting to get out.

AT WORK ... You spend most of your time wanting to get out and go inside bars.

IN PRISON ... They ball-and-chain you when you go somewhere.

AT WORK ... You are just ball-and-chained.

IN PRISON ... You get your own room.

AT WORK ... You have to share.

6

在监狱里……你的所有费用是由纳税人支付的，你都不需要用劳动来换取。

上班时……你得支付为了去上班而产生的所有费用。另外还要从你的工资中扣除税款以支付监狱里那些犯人的费用。

在监狱里……大部分时间里，你透过栅栏望向外面想要出去。

上班时……大部分时间里，你想着出来到酒吧里去。

在监狱里……你只有在要去某些地方时才会被带上镣铐。

上班时……你就是被禁锢了。

在监狱里……你拥有一个单间。

上班时……你得和别人共处一室。

IN PRISON . . . You can join many programs which you can leave at any time.

AT WORK . . . There are some programs you can never get out of.

IN PRISON . . . There are wardens who are often sadistic.

AT WORK . . . You have managers.

IN PRISON . . . You have unlimited time to read jokes.

AT WORK . . . You get fired if you get caught.

上班这件事

8

在监狱里……你可以参加很多活动，而且可以随时离开。

上班时……总有些活动避无可避。

在监狱里……有些看守是施虐狂。

上班时……你是有上司的。

在监狱里……你有的是时间看笑话。

上班时……如果你看笑话被抓到的话就会被炒鱿鱼。

☆ **cubicle** /ˈkjuːbɪkl/ *n.* 小房间；隔间

☆ **bar** /bɑː(r)/ *n.* （用作栅栏等的）杆，棒；酒吧间

☆ **sadistic** /səˈdɪstɪk/ *a.* 【心】施虐狂的

Good First Impression

A young doctor was just setting up his first office. He had just rented a beautiful office and had it furnished with equipment and fittings.

Then his secretary told him there was a man to see him. The doctor wanted to make a good first impression by having the man think he was successful and very busy. He told his secretary to show the man in.

At that moment, the doctor picked up the telephone and pretended to be having a conversation with a patient. The man waited silently until the "conversation" was over. Then, the doctor put the telephone down and asked the visitor, "Can I help you?"

To which the man replied, "No, I'm just here to connect your telephone."

上班这件事

工事中

10

良好的第一印象

一个年轻医生刚刚开设了自己的第一家诊所。他刚刚租下一间漂亮的办公室，并布置好器具陈设。

这时秘书告诉他有人找他。年轻人想给来人一个良好的第一印象，使人认为自己是工作繁忙的成功人士。他让秘书把来人领进来。

这时，他自己拿起话筒，假装在和病人通电话。那个人一声不吭地等他把"电话"打完。然后，医生放下话筒问道："你要看病吗？"

那个人回答："不，我是来给你接电话线的。"

Send Him the Account

A doctor and a lawyer were attending a cocktail party when the doctor was approached by a man who asked advice on how to handle his stomach ulcer. The doctor mumbled some medical advice, then turned to the lawyer and asked, "How do you handle the situation when you are asked for advice during a social function?"

"Just send an account for such advice," replied the lawyer.

On the next morning the doctor arrived at his surgery and issued the stomach-ulcer-stricken man a $60 account.

That afternoon he received a $100 account from the lawyer.

把账单寄给他

一位医生和一名律师在参加一个鸡尾酒会。这时，一个人走上前来问医生怎样缓解他的胃溃疡。医生含混不清地说了几句，然后转向律师问道："像这种在公共场合向你咨询的情况，你是怎么处理的？"

"我会把咨询费的账单寄给他，"律师答。

第二天早上，医生一到诊所就签了一张 60 元的账单寄给那个胃溃疡的人。

当天下午，他收到了律师寄来的 100 元咨询费账单。

☆ **ulcer** /ˈʌlsə(r)/ *n.*【医】溃疡

☆ **mumble** /ˈmʌmbl/ *v.* 含糊地说，咕哝

The Workers' Prayer

Grant me the serenity to accept the things I cannot change，the courage to change the things I cannot accept，and the wisdom to hide the bodies of those people I had to kill today because they pissed me off.

Help me to be careful of the toes I step on today as they may be connected to the behind that I may have to kiss tomorrow.

Help me to always give 100% at work....
12% on Mondays
23% on Tuesdays
40% on Wednesdays

上班这件事

工事中

14

上班人的祈祷文

对于我无法改变的事情，请赐予我平和；在我想要改变我不能接受的事情时，请赐予我勇气；另外，今天有人惹火了我，我非杀了他不可，请赐予我藏匿尸身的智慧。

请帮助我注意现在不要得罪人，因为也许明天他就会变成我不得不要巴结的人。

请帮助我让我百分百地投入工作——

（具体分配如下）

星期一 12%

星期二 23%

星期三 40%

20% on Thursdays

5% on Fridays

And help me to remember. . . .

When I'm having a really bad day, and it seems that people are trying to piss me off, that it takes 42 muscles to frown and only 4 to extend my finger and smack them on the face!

Now get back to work!

上
班
这
件
事

工事中

星期四 20%

星期五 5%

同时请帮助我永远记得……

当我度过难过的一天是因为有人找我麻烦时，皱皱眉头需要调动 42 块肌肉，而伸伸手掴他个耳光却只需要动用 4 块肌肉！

现在回去工作吧！

☆ **serenity** /sɪˈrenətɪ/ *n.* 平静；安详

☆ **piss off**　使厌烦；使恼火

☆ **step on sb.'s toes**　得罪某人

☆ **kiss sb.'s behind** 拍某人马屁，谄媚巴结某人

I Don't Have to

The boss returned from lunch in a good mood and called the whole staff in to listen to a couple of jokes he had picked up.

Everybody, but one young man laughed uproariously.

"What's the matter?" grumbled the boss. "Haven't you got a sense of humor?"

"I don't have to laugh," he smiled and replied. "I'm leaving tomorrow."

18

我没必要

老板吃完午饭回来，心情很好，就把员工们叫到一起听他讲几个刚听来的笑话。

所有人都哄然大笑，除了一个年轻人。

"怎么回事？"老板很不满，"难道你没有幽默感吗？"

"我没必要笑，"他微笑着答道，"我明天就走了。"

☆ **uproariously** /ʌpˈrɔːriəsli/ *ad.* 喧嚣地；热闹地

☆ **grumble** /ˈɡrʌmbl/ *v.* 抱怨；对…表示不满

I'm Not a Quitter

A young lady came in for her interview with the human resources department of a large company and handed the executive her application.

As the executive began to scan her resume, he noticed that she had been fired from every job she'd ever held.

"I must say," said the executive, "your work history is terrible. You've been fired from every job."

"Yes," said the lady.

"Well," continued the executive, "there's not much positive in that."

"Well," said the woman as she poked the application. "At least I'm not a quitter!"

上
班
这
件
事

工事中

我不是轻易放弃的人

一位年轻的女士到一家大公司应聘面试，她把自己的材料递给人力资源部总监。

总监检视她的材料时发现之前她做的每份工作都以被解雇告终。

"我不得不说，"总监说，"你的履历实在是太差了，每次都是你被解雇。"

"是这样的，"她说。

"呃，"总监继续说，"这其中实在没什么积极的因素。"

"可是，"她戳着申请材料说，"至少我不是轻易放弃的人！"

I Know

A witness to an automobile accident was testifying. The lawyer asked him, "Did you actually see the accident?"

The witness, "Yes, sir."

The lawyer, "How far away were you when the accident happened?"

The witness, "Twenty-nine feet, eight and one quarter inches."

The lawyer smiled (thinking he'd trap the witness), "Well, sir, will you tell the jury how you knew it was exactly that distance?"

The witness, "Because when the accident happened I took out a tape and measured it. I knew some annoying lawyer would ask me that question."

我知道

一场车祸的目击证人正在作证。律师问他："你确实看到了那起事故吗？"

证人答："是的，先生。"

律师："当时你距离事发地有多远？"

证人："二十九英尺，八又四分之一英寸。"

律师笑着（认为自己已经给证人下了套）问："现在，先生，请你告诉陪审团你怎么会知道这么确切的距离的？"

证人："那是因为事故一发生，我就拿了一个卷尺去量的。我知道会有某个烦人的律师问我这种问题的。"

☆ **testify** /ˈtestɪfaɪ/ *v.* 作证，证明

The Laws of Work

After any salary raise, you will have less money at the end of the month than you did before.

Don't be irreplaceable; if you can't be replaced, you can't be promoted.

Eat one live toad the first thing in the morning and nothing worse will happen to you the rest of the day.

If at first you don't succeed, try again. Then quit. No use being a complete fool about it.

If you can't get your work done in the first 24 hours, work nights.

It doesn't matter what you do; it only matters what you say you've done and what you're going to do.

工作法则

涨工资以后，你到月底兜里剩下的钱会比以前还少。

不要让自己成为不可或缺的人。因为如果那样的话，你就不会得到提升了。

每天早上一上班就去拍马屁，包你一整天过得顺顺当当。

如果一开始不能成功，再试一次，然后就放弃，没必要为此犯傻。

如果不能在第一天把工作做好，就每晚加班吧。

你做什么并不重要，重要的是你说你做过什么以及要做什么。

The more crap you put up with, the more crap you are going to get.

There will always be beer cans rolling on the floor of your car when the boss asks for a ride home from the office.

When the bosses talk about improving productivity, they are never talking about themselves.

You can go anywhere you want if you look serious and carry a clipboard.

Keep your boss's boss off your boss's back.

Everything can be filed under "miscellaneous."

Never delay the ending of a meeting or the beginning of a cocktail hour.

To err is human, to forgive is not our policy.

你忍的越多就会有更多要忍的。

老板下班要搭你的车回家时，要保证你的车厢地板上有啤酒罐滚动。

老板们在谈到提高生产效率时，总是不包括他们自己的。

当你表情肃穆而且手里拿着写字夹板的时候，你就可以去想去的任何地方。

帮你的老板躲开他的老板的监督。

所有东西都可以归入"杂项"类。

会议的结束时间和鸡尾酒会的开始时间都是不能延迟的。

犯错人皆难免，宽恕不是我们的政策。

Anyone can do any amount of work provided it isn't the work he/she is supposed to be doing.

Important letters that contain no errors will develop errors in the mail.

If you are good, you will be assigned all the work. If you are really good, you will get out of it.

People who go to conferences are the ones who shouldn't.

If it weren't for the last minute, nothing would get done.

At work, the authority of a person is inversely proportional to the number of pens that person is carrying.

When you don't know what to do, walk fast and look worried.

上班这件事

每个人都能做一定量的工作，只要这工作不是他/她该做的那份。

没有错误的重要信件在邮寄过程中会产生错误。

如果你的表现够好，所有的工作都会指派给你；如果你够精明，你就能逃避掉。

去参加会议的人往往都是不该去的人。

不到最后一分钟，什么事也做不好。

在工作中，一个人的权威性是和他拿的笔的数量成反比的。

你不知道该做什么时，就加快步伐并做出忧心忡忡的样子好了。

上班这件事

Following the rules will not get the job done.

Getting the job done is no excuse for not following the rules.

No matter how much you do, you never do enough.

The last person that quit or was fired will be held responsible for everything that goes wrong.

The first 90% of a project takes 10% of the time, the last 10% takes the other 90% of the time.

上班这件事

工事中

遵守规则并不能把工作做好。

把工作做好不能成为不遵守规则的借口。

不管做了多少，你做的总是不够的。

最后一个辞职或被解雇的人要为所有的错误负全责。

一项工作的前 90% 用掉 10% 的工时，做后 10% 的工作则要花去剩下的 90% 的工时。

☆ **irreplaceable** /ˌɪrɪˈpleɪsəbl/ *a.* 不可替代的；独一无二的

☆ **eat sb. 's toads**　拍某人马屁

☆ **nights** /naɪts/ *ad.* 每夜；在夜晚

☆ **put up with**　忍受，容忍

☆ **clipboard** /ˈklɪpbɔːd/ *n.* 带弹簧夹的写字板，写字夹板

☆ **miscellaneous** /ˌmɪsəˈleɪnɪəs/ *a.* 各色各样的

☆ **inversely** /ˈɪnvɜːs/ *ad.* 相反地；倒转地

☆ **proportional** /prəʊˈpɔːʃənl/ *a.* 比例的；成比例的

An Amazing Salesman

The manager of a department store came to check on his new salesman. In fact, it was really a megastore — you could get anything there.

"How many sales did you make today?" the manager asked.

"One," replied the new guy.

"Only one?" said the manager. "Most of my staff make some 20 sales a day. How much was the sale worth?"

The salesman answered, "$43,868."

Flabbergasted, the manager asked him to explain.

不可思议的推销员

一家百货商场的经理到店里检视新来的推销员。事实上，这是一家超大的商场，里面应有尽有，什么都能买到。

"你今天做成了几笔买卖？"经理问。

"一笔，"新来的推销员答。

"只有一笔吗？"经理说，"我们的大部分员工每天都能大约成交 20 笔呢。你卖了多少钱？"

推销员答："43 868 元。"

经理大吃一惊，要他说说看。

上班这件事

"First I sold a man a fishhook," the salesman said. "Then I sold him a rod and a reel. Then I asked where he was going fishing, and he said down by the coast. So I suggested he'd need a boat, then I took him down to the boat department. He bought a runabout. When he said his Volkswagen might not be able to pull it, I took him to the automotive department and sold him a big SUV."

The amazed manager asked, "You sold all that to a guy who came in for a fishhook?"

"No," the new salesman replied. "He actually came in for a bottle of aspirin for his wife's migraine. I told him, Your weekend's shot. You may as well go fishing."

"首先，我卖给他一个钓钩，"推销员说，"然后卖给他钓竿和线轴。接着我问他准备去哪儿钓鱼，他说要去海边。于是我就建议他买一条船，并把他带到船只部，他买了一艘小汽艇。当他说他的车装不下这汽艇时，我就把他带到汽车部，卖给他一辆大 SUV。"

惊讶的经理问道："你把所有这些东西卖给了一个来买钓钩的人？"

"不是的，"新来的推销员说，"事实上，他是因为妻子的偏头痛而来给她买阿司匹林的。我对他说：'你这个周末算是泡汤了，不如去钓鱼吧。'"

☆ **flabbergast** /ˈflæbəɡɑːst/ v.〈口〉使大吃一惊，使目瞪口呆

☆ **migraine** /ˈmiːɡreɪn/ n.【医】偏头痛

☆ **shot** /ʃɒt/ a.〈美俚〉筋疲力尽的；破旧的；毁灭的

Whose Job Is It?

This is a story about four people named Everybody, Somebody, Anybody, and Nobody.

There was an important job to be done, and Everybody was asked to do it. Everybody was sure Somebody would do it. Anybody could have done it, but Nobody did it.

Somebody got angry about that, because it was Everybody's job. Everybody thought Anybody could do it, but Nobody realized that Everybody wouldn't do it.

Consequently, it ended up that Everybody blamed Somebody when Nobody did what Anybody could have done.

上班这件事

工事中

36

这是谁的工作？

这个故事讲到了四个人，他们分别叫作每个人、有些人、任何人和没有人。

有一项重要的工作要求每个人做。每个人确信有些人会做。本来任何人可以做的，可是没有人做。

有些人对此很气愤，因为这是每个人的工作。每个人想任何人可以做，可是没有人意识到每个人都不会做。

结果，在没有人做任何人都能做的事情时，每个人都指责有些人。

☆ **consequently** /ˈkɒsɪkwəntlɪ/ *ad.* 所以，因此

☆ **blame** /bleɪm/ *v.* 指摘，责备

Neither Do I

Two young engineers applied for a single position at a computer company. They both had the same qualifications. In order to determine which individual to hire, the applicants were asked to take a test of 12 questions by the manager of human resources department.

Upon completion of the test, both men had each missed only one of the questions. The manager went to the first applicant and said, "Thank you for your interest, but we've decided to give the job to the other applicant."

"And why would you be doing that? We both got eleven questions correct," asked the rejected applicant.

我也不

两个年轻的工程师应聘一家电脑公司的同一个职位。他们的资历相当。为了决定雇用哪一个，公司的人力资源部经理要他们做一个测试——回答 12 个问题。

测试结束后，两个人各有一个问题没答上来，经理对其中的一个说："感谢你对我们公司的关注，可是我们决定聘用另一个人。"

"可是为什么呢？我们两人都答对了 11 道题呀，"不被录用的人问。

"We have based our decision not on the correct answers, but on the question you missed," said the department manager.

"And just how would one incorrect answer be better than the other?" the rejected applicant inquired.

"Simple," said the department manager, "Your fellow applicant put down on question No. 8, 'I don't know.' You put down, 'Neither do I.'"

"我们做出这个决定不是基于正确的答案，而是基于你们没有答对的那个问题，"经理答道。

　　"那么一个错误答案能比另一个错误答案好到哪里去呢？"不被录用的人问。

　　"很简单，"经理说，"另一为应聘者对于第八题的回答是'我不知道'；而你的回答是'我也不知道。'"

上班这件事

How to Get a Higher Salary

A boss tells his new employee，"I'll give you 15 bucks an hour starting today and in three months，I'll raise it to 20 bucks an hour. So when would you like to start?"

"In 3 months."

怎样得到更高的薪水

一个老板对新雇员说:"你开始工作的头三个月我给你十五元一小时,三个月后给你提到二十元一小时。你准备什么时候开始来上班?"

"三个月后。"

☆ buck /bʌk/ n. 〈美俚〉(一)元;(一笔)钱

I Just Need One Copy

A young secretary was leaving the office on her lunch break when she found the CEO（Chief Executive Officer）standing in front of a shredder with a piece of paper in hand.

She walked up to him and asked if he need help.

"Listen," said the CEO, "this is important. Can you make this thing work?"

"Certainly," said the young secretary.

She turned the machine on, inserted the paper, and pressed the start button.

"Excellent, excellent!" said the CEO as his paper disappeared inside the machine. "Thanks, I just need one copy."

我只要复印一份

午饭时间，一个年轻的秘书正要离开办公室。这时，她看见首席执行官拿着一张纸站在碎纸机前。

她走上前去问他是否需要帮助。

"听着，"首席执行官说，"这很重要。你能告诉我这东西怎么用吗？"

"当然，"秘书说。

她打开机器，把纸塞进去，然后按下"开始"按钮。

"太好了，太好了！"首席执行官看着自己那张纸消失在机器中，说："谢谢你，我只要复印一份。"

☆ **shredder** /ˈʃredə(r)/ *n.* 碎纸机

Restroom Policy

To All Employees

In the past, employees were permitted to make trips to the restroom under informal guidelines. A new Restroom Policy will be established to provide a consistent method of accounting for each employee's restroom time and ensuring equal treatment of all employees.

Under this policy, a "Restroom Trip Bank" will be established for each employee. The first day of each month, employees will be given a Restroom Trip Credit of 20 points. RTC can be accumulated from month to month.

Shortly, the entrances to all the restrooms will begin being equipped with personnel

洗手间使用政策

全体员工

过去员工可以随意去洗手间。鉴于此，我们将执行一项新的洗手间使用政策，为员工使用洗手间的时间制定了一贯的细则，并能够保证对所有员工一视同仁。

根据本政策规定，我们将为每位员工建立一个"洗手间使用账户"。每个月的第一天，账户中将充入"洗手间使用余额"20 点。该点数可以逐月累积。

不久以后，所有的洗手间的入门处都将安装员工身份认证以及与电脑连接的声音识别系统。在接

identification stations and computer linked voice print recognition. During the next two (2) weeks, each employee must provide two copies of voiceprints (one normal and one under stress).

If an employee's RTB balances at zero (0), the doors to all restrooms will not unlock for that employee's voice print until the first day of the month.

In addition, all the restrooms are being equipped with a time paper roll retractor. If the restroom is occupied for more than three (3) minutes, an alarm will sound throughout the entire building. A computer simulated voice will be activated and announce over the public announcing system the name of the delinquent employee.

上班这件事

48

下来的两个星期中，每位员工要提供两份声纹（一份正常情况下的，一份紧张时的）。

如果某位员工的"洗手间使用账户"的余额为零，那么在下个月的第一天到来之前，他的声纹将不能打开所有洗手间的门。

另外，所有的洗手间里的卷筒纸都配有定时缩回装置。如果有人使用洗手间超过3分钟，整个大楼里都将响起警报，电脑的声音系统将被激活向大家公布这位懈怠的员工的姓名。

Ten (10) seconds later, the roll of paper will retract, the toilet will flush and the restroom door will automatically open. If at that time, the employee still remains seated inside the stall, the restroom cameras (which will be linked to the payroll and security console) will turn on.

Your cooperation on this matter will be appreciated. If you have any questions about the new policy, please feel free to ask your supervisor.

Thank You!

Management

上班这件事

工事中

50

10 秒钟后，卷筒纸将会缩回，马桶将会冲水，洗手间的门也将随之自动打开。如果到那时，这位员工仍然坐在隔间里，洗手间的照相装置（与员工薪水名册挂钩并连接到安保系统）将被打开。

感谢你们对此项政策的支持与合作。有任何问题可向你们的上级询问。

谢谢！

管理层

☆ **consistent** /kən'sɪstənt/ *a*. 坚持的；一贯的

☆ **delinquent** /dɪ'lɪŋkwənt/ *a*. 失职的，懈怠的

☆ **payroll** /'peɪrəul/ *n*. 工资表；在职人员名单

☆ **console** /kən'səul/ *n*. 控制台，操纵台

Blonde Looking for a Job

A blonde was filling out an application form for a job.

She promptly filled the columns entitled NAME，AGE，ADDRESS，etc.

Then she came to the column: SALARY EXPECTED.

"Yes."

金发女郎找工作记

一个金发女郎找工作时填一张申请表格。

表格中要求填写的诸如"姓名"、"年龄"、"地址"等项，她很快都填完了。

接着她看到这一项："期望薪金"。

于是她在空格处填上"是的"。

上班这件事

53

Why I Am So Tired

For a couple years I've been blaming it on lack of vitamins, dieting and a dozen other maladies. Now I found out the real reason. I'm tired because I'm overworked.

The population of this country is 237 million. 104 million are retired. That leaves 133 million to do the work.

There are 85 million in school, which leave 48 million to do the work.

Of this, there are 29 million employed by the federal government. This leaves 19 million to do the work.

Four million are in the Armed Forces, which leaves 15 million to do the work.

我为什么这么累

好几年了，我一直认为自己总是感到疲劳是由于缺乏维生素、节食和一大堆病的缘故。现在我终于把真实的原因搞明白了——我累是因为我工作过度了。

这个国家一共有两亿三千七百万的人口，其中有一亿零四百万的人退休了，这样就剩下一亿三千三百万人工作了。

这其中有八千五百万的人还在上学，这样就剩下四千八百万人工作了。

这其中又有两千九百万受雇于联邦政府，这样就剩下一千九百万人工作了。

这其中又有四百万在军中服役，这样就剩下一千五百万人工作了。

Take from the total the 14,800,000 people who work for State and City Government and that leaves 200,000 to do the work.

There are 188,000 in hospitals, so that leaves 12,000 to do the work.

Now, there are 11,998 people in Prisons. That leaves just two people to do the work.

You and me . . .

And you're sitting there reading jokes!

No wonder I'm tired; I'm doing ALL of the work myself!

除去受雇于各州和市政府的一千四百八十万人，就剩下二十万人工作了。

这其中又有十八万八千人在住院，这样就剩下一万二千人工作了。

现在有一万一千九百九十八人关在监狱里，这样就剩下两个人工作了。

你和我……

而你却坐在那儿看笑话！

难怪我这么累了，我一个人干了所有的工作！

☆ **blame** /bleɪm/ *v.* 归咎于

☆ **malady** /ˈmælədɪ/ *n.* 疾病（尤指慢性病或痼疾）

That's Your Worry

Fresh out of business school, the young man answered a want ad for an accountant.

Now he was being interviewed by a highly agitated, arrogant little man who ran a small business that he had started from scratch.

"I need someone with an accounting degree," the man said. "But mainly, I'm looking for someone to do my worrying for me."

"How's that?" the would-be accountant asked.

"I worry about a lot of things," the man said. "But I don't want to have to worry about money. Your job will be to take all the money worries off my back."

那是你的事情

一个年轻人刚从商业学校毕业，去一家小公司应聘做会计。

现在他正在被一个焦躁而傲慢的小个子男人面试，这间公司就是他刚刚白手起家办起来的。

"我需要一个有会计学学位的人，"小个子男人说，"可是，最重要的是，我要找的是能为我分忧的人。"

"那是什么意思？"年轻人问道。

"我要操心很多事情，"那人说，"但是我不想再为钱的事情操心了，你的工作就是替我分担这些对钱的操心。"

上班这件事

"I see," the accountant said. "And how much will my position pay?"

"I'll start you at eighty five thousand," responded the man decisively.

" Eighty five thousand dollars!" the accountant exclaimed. "How can such a small business afford a sum like that?"

"That," the man said, "is your first worry. Now get to work!"

上班这件事

工事中

"我明白了，"年轻人说，"那么我的工资是多少？"

"你的起薪是 85000 块，"那人语气肯定地说。

"85000 元！"年轻人大声说，"这样一间小公司怎么能付得起这样高的工资？"

那人说："这就是你首先要操心的事。现在开始工作吧！"

☆ **agitated** /ˈædʒɪteɪtɪd/ *a.* 狂躁不安的；焦虑的

☆ **arrogant** /ˈærəgənt/ *a.* 傲慢的；自大的

☆ **from scratch** 从起点开始；从头做起

☆ **worry** /ˈwʌrɪ/ *n.* 某人负责的事情

Your Last Question

A new client had just come in to see a famous lawyer.

"Can you tell me how much you charge?" said the client.

"Of course," the lawyer replied, "I charge $200 to answer three questions!"

"Well that's a bit steep, isn't it?"

"Yes it is," said the lawyer, "And what's your third question?"

你的最后一个问题

一个新客户去见一位知名的律师。

他问道："请告诉我你怎么收费，好吗？"

"当然，"律师答道，"回答三个问题我收费 200 元！"

"可是真够贵的啊？"

"是的，"律师说，"你的第三个问题是什么？"

☆ **steep** /sti:p/ *a.* 〈口〉（要求、价格等）过高的

上班这件事

Good News & Bad News

There's the sad story of the poor guy who was in a terrible motorcycle accident. When he came out from under the anesthetic, the doctor was leaning over him anxiously.

"Son," he said, "I've got some good news and some bad news.

"The bad news is that you were in a very serious accident, and I'm afraid we had to amputate both your feet just above the ankle."

"Jesus," gasped the patient. "What's the good news?"

"The fellow in the next bed over would like to buy your boots."

上班这件事

好消息和坏消息

一个可怜的家伙骑摩托时出了车祸。等他从麻醉中苏醒过来后，医生愁容满面地俯下身。

"孩子，我有一个好消息和一个坏消息要告诉你。"

"坏消息是你在车祸中受了重伤，我不得不把你的双腿从脚踝上面截掉。"

"天哪，"他呼吸急促地说，"好消息是什么？"

"隔壁床位的小伙子想要买你的靴子。"

☆ **anesthetic** /ˌænɪs'θetɪk/ *n.* 麻醉药，麻醉剂

☆ **amputate** /'æmpjuteɪt/ *v.* 截（肢）

☆ **gasp** /gɑːsp/ *v.* 喘着气说出

The Retirement Party

The manager was finally old enough to retire from the company.

On his last day of work, he ordered a farewell party for himself. The manager wanted everyone to express their good feeling about him by writing on the farewell card, so later he could remember how his staff "miss" him.

Most people are writing standard phrases like, "Without you, the company will never be the same," "We will always remember you," etc.

Obviously the manager was not satisfied.

"I need something from the bottom of your heart, something really touching, you know. Okay, John, you have been working with me for the last 20 years. You are my best staff. I am retiring now. What do you have to say?"

Slowly but firmly, John wrote, "THE BEST NEWS IN 20 YEARS."

退休欢送会

公司经理到了该退休的年龄。

上班的最后一天，他给自己举办了一个欢送会。他要每个人写一张告别卡片，写上对他的好的感想。这样，在退休后的日子里他就能感受到员工们是怎样地"想念"他。

大多数人都中规中矩地写了诸如"没有你，公司就不一样了"或是"我们会永远记得你"之类的话。

可是显然经理对这些并不满意。

"我需要一些发自内心的、真正感人的东西。好，约翰，你跟着我干了 20 年，你是我最得意的员工。现在我要退休了。你该说点儿什么吧?"

约翰写得很慢，但是毫不迟疑——"20 年来最好的消息。"

67

Rules to Give to Your Boss

Rules for Work（Should go over well with your boss.）

Print it out and hang it over your workstation....

1. Never give me work in the morning. Always wait until 4 : 00 and then bring it to me. The challenge of a deadline is refreshing.

2. If it's really a rush job, run in and interrupt me every 10 minutes to inquire how it's going. That helps. Or even better, hover behind me, and advise me at every keystroke.

3. Always leave without telling anyone where you're going. It gives me a chance to be creative when someone asks where you are.

4. If my arms are full of papers, boxes,

给你老板的规定

工作条例（应得到老板的赞许）

把它打印出来张贴在办公室里。

1. 不要在早上给我布置工作。要等到下午 4 点钟再说，挑战最后期限的工作才有意思。

2. 如果这是一份紧急工作，就每十分钟跑进来打断我问一下进展。这很有帮助的。或者可以更甚，就在我身后转悠，我每干点儿什么就提点儿建议。

3. 你要出去时，不要告诉任何人。这样，当有人问起你时，我的回答就可以很有创造性。

4. 如果我手上抱满了纸张、盒子、书本或是

books, or office supplies, don't open the door for me. I need to learn how to function as a paraplegic and opening doors with no arms is good training in case I should ever be injured and lose all use of my limbs.

5. If you give me more than one job to do, don't tell me which is priority. I am psychic.

6. Do your best to keep me late. I adore this office and really have nowhere to go or anything to do. I have no life beyond work.

7. If a job I do pleases you, keep it a secret. If that gets out, it could mean a promotion.

8. If you don't like my work, tell everyone. I like my name to be popular in conversations. I was born to be whipped.

9. If you have special instructions for a job, don't write them down. In fact, save them until

办公用品，不要帮我开门。我该学学像残疾人一样生活。不用手开门就是很好的训练，这样，万一我受伤失去手臂就没问题了。

5. 如果你一次交代给我几件事做，不要告诉我哪件更重要，我有心灵感应。

6. 尽你所能让我加班吧。我热爱这间公司，而且我真的没地方可去也没事可做。工作就是我生活的全部。

7. 如果我的工作做得让你满意，不要说出来。如果说出来，就意味着要提升我了。

8. 如果我的工作做得让你不满意，就说出来吧。我喜欢同事们谈论我，我生来就是挨批的。

9. 如果你对某项工作有特别的指示，不要写给我。就留到工作快要做完时再对我说吧。没必要用些有用的信息来困惑我。

the job is almost done. No use confusing me with useful information.

10. Never introduce me to the people you're with. I have no right to know anything. In the corporate food chain, I am plankton. When you refer to them later, my shrewd deductions will identify them.

11. Tell me all your little problems. It's nice to know someone is less fortunate. I especially like the story about having to pay so many taxes on the bonus check you received for being such a good manager.

12. Wait until my yearly review and THEN tell me what my goals SHOULD have been. Give me a mediocre performance rating with a cost of living increase. I'm not here for the money anyway.

10. 不要把我介绍给和你在一起的人，我没有权利知道任何事情。在公司组织中，我处于最底层。今后，你再提到他们时，我自然会敏锐地推导出谁是谁。

11. 把你遇到的小问题都告诉我。知道有人不那么幸运的感觉很好。我尤其喜欢听那段，就是关于你这个成功的经理要为你拿到的大笔红利缴纳高额税费。

12. 到我该做年终检查时再告诉我本年度的目标是什么。给我一个不好不坏的评定，还有提高一点儿生活费用，毕竟我在这儿工作不是为了钱的。

☆ **go over**　获得成功；得到赞许

☆ **refreshing** /rɪˈfreʃɪŋ/ *a.* 给人新鲜感的

☆ **hover** /ˈhɒvə(r)/ *v.* 逗留在近旁；徘徊

☆ **paraplegic** /ˌpærəˈpliːdʒɪk/ *n.* 截瘫患者，下身麻痹者

☆ **priority** /praɪˈɒrətɪ/ *n.* 重点；优先考虑的事

☆ **psychic** /ˈsaɪkɪk/ *a.* 精神的；超自然的

☆ **plankton** /ˈplæŋktən/ *n.* [总称] 浮游生物

☆ **mediocre** /ˌmiːdɪˈəʊkə(r)/ *a.* 中等的，平庸的

Where Were You Yesterday?

John had this problem of getting up late in the morning and was always late for work.

His boss was mad at him and threatened to fire him if he didn't do something about it. So John went to his doctor who gave him a pill and told him to take it before he went to bed.

John slept well and in fact beat the alarm in the morning by almost two hours.

He had a leisurely breakfast and drove cheerfully to work.

"Boss," John said, "The pill actually worked!"

"That's all fine," said the boss. "But where were you yesterday?"

昨天你上哪儿去了？

约翰早上总是起不来床，所以上班经常迟到。

他的老板对此非常恼火，就威胁他如果不能有所改变的话就炒掉他。于是约翰去看了医生，医生给了他一种药片，要他睡觉前服下。

约翰甜美地睡了一觉而且提前了近两个小时就醒了。

他从从容容地吃了一顿早饭，然后开心地开车上班去了。

"老板，"约翰说，"那药真的管用了！"

"很好。"老板说，"可是，你昨天干什么去了？"

Wanna Buy Some Mouthwash

A neatly dressed salesman stopped a man in the street and asked, "Sir, would you like to buy a bottle of this mouthwash for $160?"

Aghast, the man said, "Are you NUTS? That's robbery!"

The salesman seemed hurt and then tries again, "Sir, since you are a bit irate, I'll sell it to you for half price at $80?"

Again, the man replies bluntly, "You must be crazy, now go away!"

The salesman then reaches into his briefcase and pulls out two hotdogs and begins

想买漱口水

一个衣着整洁的街头推销员拦住了一个路人问道："先生，买一瓶漱口水好吗？160 元。"

那人吓了一跳，说道："你疯了吗？这简直就是抢钱！"

推销员做出受了伤害的样子，继续试道："先生，既然您生气了，那么我半价卖给您好不好？"

那人直截了当地答道："你疯了，走开！"

于是推销员从包里拿出两个热狗，津津有味地

munching on one of them. He told the irate guy,
"Sir, please share one of my hotdogs since I
have annoyed you so much."

The guy takes a bite; suddenly, he spits it
out and snarled, "HEY, this hotdog tastes like
crap!!!"

"It is," replied the salesman, smiled.
"Now wanna buy some mouthwash?"

吃起一个来。他对那人说："先生，我惹您生气了，请分享一个我的热狗吧。"

那人咬了一口，马上就吐了出来，叫道："这玩意儿吃起来就像是在吃屎！！！"

"是的，"推销员微笑着答道，"现在想买漱口水吗？"

☆ **aghast** /ə'gɑːst/ *a.* 吓呆的；惊骇的

☆ **nuts** /nʌts/ *a.* 发疯的；发狂的

☆ **irate** /aɪ'reɪt/ *a.* 发怒的，愤怒的

☆ **bluntly** /'blʌntlɪ/ *ad.* 率直地；生硬地

☆ **munch** /mʌntʃ/ *v.* 用力咀嚼；津津有味地嚼

☆ **snarl** /snɑːl/ *v.* 咆哮

Here's My Answers

In most offices, the photocopier is out of order every now and then. One copy repairman had answered question after question for the employees.

Finally one day, he just smiled and handed them this sheet.

The copier is out of order!

Yes, we have called the service man.

Yes, he will be in today.

No, we cannot fix it.

No, we do not know how long it will take.

No, we do not know what caused it.

No, we do not know who broke it.

Yes, we are keeping it.

No, we do not know what you are going to do now.

Thank you.

这是我的回答

　　大多数公司的复印机会时不时地出些故障。一个复印机维修工不得不没完没了地回答这些公司员工们的各种问题。

　　终于有一天，他只是微笑着递给他们一张纸条，上面写着：

　　这台复印机坏了！

　　是的，我们已经叫了维修人员。

　　是的，他今天就会来。

　　不，我们修不了。

　　不，我们不知道修好它要用多长时间。

　　不，我们不知道是什么原因引起的。

　　不，我们不知道谁弄坏的。

　　是的，我们在修。

　　不，我们不知道你们现在该怎么办。

　　谢谢。

Me vs. My Boss

When I take a long time — I am slow.

When my boss takes a long time — He is thorough.

When I don't do it — I am lazy.

When my boss doesn't do it — He is too busy.

When I do something without being told — I am trying to be smart or overstepping my authority.

When my boss does the same — That is initiative.

When I please my boss — I'm apple-polishing.

When my boss pleases his boss — He's co-operating.

我和我的老板

我用了很长时间——我太慢。

我老板用了很长时间——他工作仔细。

我不做——懒。

我老板不做——他太忙。

我做了没要求我做的事情——我在耍小聪明或是越权。

我老板做了没要求他做的事情——他是积极上进。

我讨好我的老板时——我是在拍马屁。

我老板讨好他的老板时——他是在配合工作。

上班这件事

When I do good — My boss never remembers.

When I do wrong — He never forgets.

When I make a mistake — I'm an idiot.

When my boss makes a mistake — He's only human.

When I take a stand — I'm being bullheaded.

When my boss does it — He's being firm.

When I overlook a rule of etiquette — I'm being rude.

When my boss skips a few rules — He's being original.

When I'm out of the office — I'm wandering around.

When my boss is out of the office — He's on business.

我做得好的——我老板从来不记得。

我做错了的——我老板从来不会忘记。

我犯了错误——我是个白痴。

我老板犯了错误——他也是人嘛。

当我表明立场时——我在犯傻。

我老板这样做时——他是很沉稳。

当我忽视了某些规矩时——我很无礼。

当我老板不遵从某些规则时——他是在创新。

我不在公司时——我就是在闲逛。

我老板不在公司时——他是在办公事。

When I'm on a day off sick — I'm always sick.

When my boss is a day off sick — He must be very ill.

When I apply for leave — I must be going for an interview.

When my boss applies for leave — It's because he's overworked.

上班这件事

工事中

86

我请一天病假——我总是生病。

我老板请一天病假——他一定病得不轻。

我请假——我一定去面试了。

我老板请假——因为他工作过度。

☆ **overstep** /ˌəʊvəˈstep/ *v.* 超越；侵越

☆ **initiative** /ɪˈvɪteɪʃɪnɪʃiɪtɪv/ *n.* 首创精神；进取心

☆ **apple-polish** /ˈæplˌpɒlɪʃ/ *v.* 〈美俚〉逢迎，拍马屁

☆ **take a stand**　表明立场（意见、态度等）

☆ **bullheaded** /ˈbʊlˌhedɪd/ *a.* 蠢笨的；鲁莽的

☆ **etiquette** /ˈetɪket/ *n.* （行业中的）道德规矩；
　沿习

How Many Vice Presidents

Tom was so excited about his promotion to Vice President of the company he worked for and kept bragging about it to his wife for weeks on end.

Finally she couldn't take it any longer, and told him, "Listen, it means nothing, they even have a vice president of peas at the grocery store!"

"Really?" Not sure if this was true or not, Tom decided to call the grocery store.

A clerk answers and Tom says, "Can I please talk to the Vice President of peas?"

The clerk replies, "Canned or frozen?"

上班这件事

有多少副主管

汤姆被提升为公司的副主管，他兴奋极了，连着几个星期对妻子自我夸耀着。

她终于受不了了，对他说："听着，这没什么了不起的。杂货店里卖豌豆的还有副主管呢！"

"真的吗？"不知道她说的是不是真事，汤姆决定给杂货店打个电话。

一个店员接了电话，汤姆说，"我想找一下你们的豌豆副主管，行吗？"

店员问："你要找罐头的还是冷冻的？"

☆ **brag** /bræg/ *v.* 自夸，吹嘘

☆ **on end** 连续地

What If. . . .

Tom is applying for a job as a signalman for the local railroad.

The inspector decides to give Tom a quiz, asking, "What would you do if you realized that two trains were heading towards each other on the same track?"

Tom says, "I would switch one train to another track."

"What if the lever broke?" asks the inspector.

"I'd run down to the tracks and use the manual lever," answers Tom.

"What if that had been struck by lightning?" challenges the inspector.

如果……怎么样

汤姆在应聘做地方铁路系统的信号员。

督察决定考考他，于是问道，"如果你意识到两列火车正在同一条轨道上面对面行驶，你会怎么做？"

汤姆答："我会把其中的一列转到另一条轨道。"

"如果控制杆不起作用了呢？"督察接着问道。

汤姆答："我会跑到轨道边用手动控制杆搬动道岔。"

"如果手动控制杆遭雷击坏了呢？"督察继续考验他。

"Then," Tom continues, "I'd run back up here and use the phone to call the next signal box."

"What if the phone was busy?"

"In that case," Tom argues, "I'd run to the street level and use the public phone near the station."

"What if that had been vandalized?"

"Oh, well," says Tom, "in that case I'd run back home and get my grandpa."

This puzzles the inspector, so he asks, "Why would you do that?"

"Because he's 78 years of age but has never seen a train crash!"

"那么，"汤姆接着说，"我会跑回来打电话通知下一个信号房。"

"如果电话占线怎么办？"

"那样的话，"汤姆争辩道，"我会跑到街上打车站旁边的公用电话。"

"如果那里的电话坏了呢？"

"这样啊，"汤姆说，"如果是这样我就会跑回家把我爷爷叫来。"

这下督察不明白了，问道："你为什么要这么做？"

"因为我爷爷 78 岁了，可还没见过火车相撞呢！"

☆ **vandalize** /ˈvændəlaɪz/ *v.* 肆意毁坏

If He Hadn't Been Sick

Negotiations between union members and their employer were at an impasse. The union denied that their workers were flagrantly abusing their contract's sick-leave provisions.

One morning at the bargaining table, the company's chief negotiator held the morning edition of the newspaper.

"Look, this man," he announced, "called in sick yesterday!"

There on the sports page, was a photo of the supposedly ill employee, who had just won a local golf tournament with an excellent score.

The silence in the room was broken by a union negotiator.

"Wow," he said. "Just think of what kind of score he could have had if he hadn't been sick!"

上班这件事

工事中

94

要是他没病

工会成员和雇主的谈判陷入了僵局。工会否认工人们明目张胆地滥用了他们合同中的病假条款。

一天早上，在谈判台前，公司方的首席谈判代表拿起一份早报。

"看哪，"他大声说，"这个人昨天请了病假！"

体育版上，刊登着那个请了病假的人的照片，他刚以不错的成绩赢了高尔夫球赛。

一个工会谈判代表打破了沉默。

"哇，"他说，"想想吧，要是他没生病的话会拿到多高的分数呢！"

☆ **impasse** /ɪmˈpɑːs/ *n.* 绝境；僵局

☆ **flagrantly** /ˈfleɪgrənt/ *ad.* 罪恶昭彰地；明目张胆地

☆ **abuse** /əˈbjuːz/ *v.* 滥用，妄用

☆ **provision** /prəʊˈvɪʒən/ *n.* 条文，规定

The Reality

A company employee found an old brass lamp in a filing cabinet. When he dusted it off, a genie appeared and granted him three wishes.

"I'd love an ice-cold beer right now," he told the genie.

Poof! A beer appeared.

Next the man said, "I wish to be on a beautiful island, surrounded by beautiful women."

Poof! He was on an island with gorgeous women fawning all over him.

"Oh, man, this is the life," the guy thought. "I wish I never had to work again."

And poof . . .

He was back at his desk in the office!

现　实

一个公司职员在一个文件柜中发现了一盏古老的铜灯。他把它擦干净后，一个精灵出现了，而且能为他实现三个愿望。

"我现在就想要一罐冰啤酒，"他对精灵说。

噗的一下！一罐啤酒出现在他眼前。

接着他又说："我想在一个美丽的海岛上，有很多漂亮的女人陪着我。"

噗的一下！他已经置身在海岛上，极漂亮的女人们奉迎在旁。

"啊，这才是生活嘛，"他想着，"我要是再不用工作就好了。"

噗的一下……

他回到了公司的办公桌前！

☆ **fawn** /fɔːn/ *v.* 奉承，讨好

The New CEO

A company, feeling it was time for a shakeup, hires a new CEO. This new boss is determined to rid the company of all slackers.

On a tour of the facilities, the CEO notices a guy leaning on the doorframe with his arms folded on his chest. The room is full of workers and he thinks this is his chance to show everyone he means business!

The CEO, walks up the guy and asks, "And how much money do you make a week?"

Undaunted, the young fellow looks at him and replies, "I make $200 a week. Why?"

新来的首席执行官

一个公司在一次人事变革中雇用了新的首席执行官。而他在上任之初就决定将所有惰于工作的人都清理出去。

在一次巡视中，他注意到一个人靠在门框上，手臂交叉在胸前。屋里全是工作人员，于是他认为这是一次绝佳的机会，让每个人都知道他是说一不二的。

他走到那人跟前问道："你一个星期的工钱是多少？"

那小伙子并不怕他，看着他答道："我一星期赚 200 块钱，怎么啦？"

The CEO then hands the guy $200 in cash and screams, "Here's a week's pay, now GET OUT and DON'T come back!"

Feeling pretty good about his first firing, the CEO looks around the room and asks, "Does anyone want to tell me what that slacker did here?"

With a sheepish grin, one of the other workers mutters, "Pizza delivery guy."

上班这件事

100

新来的首席执行官递给他 200 块钱，叫道："这是你一周的工钱，拿着它走吧，不要再来了！"

第一次落实了自己的政策，新来的首席执行官自我感觉不错，他环顾四周，问道："有谁能告诉我那个偷懒的人原来是干什么的？"

一个工作人员局促地笑了一下，喃喃道："送比萨外卖的。"

☆ **shakeup** /ˈʃeɪkʌp/ *n.* （政策等的）剧变；（人员的）大改组

☆ **slacker** /ˈslækə(r)/ *n.* 偷懒的人

☆ **mean business** 〈口〉是认真的；将一定采取行动

☆ **undaunted** /ʌnˈdɔːntɪd/ *a.* 无畏的，大胆的

☆ **sheepish** /ˈʃiːpɪʃ/ *a.* 羞怯的；局促不安的

☆ **mutter** /ˈmʌtə(r)/ *v.* 小声而含糊不清地说

The New Doctor

A woman went to doctor's office. She was seen by one of the new doctors, but after about 5 minutes in the examination room, she burst out, screaming as she ran down the hall. An older doctor stopped and asked her what the problem was, and she explained. He had her sit down and relax in another room.

The older doctor marched back to the first and demanded, "What's the matter with you? Mrs. Johnson is 67 years old, she has three grown children and eight grandchildren, and you told her she was pregnant?"

The new doctor smiled smugly as he continued to write on his clipboard.

"Cured her hiccups though, didn't it?"

新来的医生

一个女人去看病。一位新来的医生为她诊察，可是进了诊疗室大约 5 分钟之后，她就尖叫着冲到大厅里。一位老医生拦住她问明情况，安排她坐到另一个房间里休息。

然后老医生大步走到新医生面前质问道："你有什么毛病没有？约翰逊夫人 67 岁了，有三个成年子女和八个孙辈。而你竟然对她说她怀孕了？"

新医生一边继续填写自己的诊疗记录，一边洋洋得意地笑着说——

"不管怎么样，我治好了她的打嗝，不是吗？"

☆ **smugly** /ˈsmʌglɪ/ *ad*. 沾沾自喜地，自鸣得意地

☆ **clipboard** /ˈklɪpbɔːd/ *n*. 写字夹板

☆ **hiccup** /ˈhɪkʌp/ *n*. 打嗝儿

The SUPER Salesman

A man walks into an insurance office one morning and asks for a job.

"Sorry, we don't need anyone ..." the manager replied.

"You can't afford not to hire me. I can sell anyone anything anytime!"

"Well, we have two prospects that no one has been able to sell. If you can sell just one, then you have a job."

He was gone about three hours and returned and handed them two checks, one for $35,000 and another for $65,000.

"How in the world did you do that?" the manager asked.

超级推销员

一天早上，一个人走进一间保险公司找工作。

"不好意思，我们现在不招人……"经理回答说。

"你们可不能舍弃我这样的人才，我可以在任何时候把任何东西卖给任何人！"

"好吧，我们有两个目标客户，可是没人能成功地让他们投保。如果你能做成其中一个，你就能得到这份工作。"

他去了三个小时，回来时手里拿着两张支票，一张三万五千元，一张六万五千元。

"你到底是怎么做到的？"经理问。

"I told you I'm the world's best salesman, I can sell anyone anything anytime!"

"Then did you get a urine sample?" the manager asked him.

"What's that?" he asked.

"Well, if you sell a policy over $30,000 the company requires a urine sample. Now take these two bottles and go back and get urine samples."

He was gone about 5 hours and the office was about to close, when he walks in with two five gallon buckets, one in each hand. He sets the buckets down on the ground and produces two bottles of urine from his shirt pocket and sets them on the desk and says, "Here's Mr. Clinton's and this one is Mr. Robinson's."

"我告诉过你我是天底下最棒的推销员，我可以在任何时候把任何东西卖给任何人！"

"那么你拿尿样了吗？"经理又问道。

"那是什么？"他问。

"是这样的，公司规定做成超过三万元的保单要留取尿样。拿这两个瓶子去取尿样吧。"

这次，他去了五个小时，公司要下班时，他一手拎着一个五加仑的桶走了进来。他把桶放在地上，然后从衬衫口袋里掏出两只瓶子放在桌子上，说道："这是克林顿先生和鲁滨逊先生的尿样。"

"That's good," the manager said, "but what's in those two buckets?"

"Well, I passed by the school house and they were having a state teachers convention, so I stopped and sold them a group policy!"

上班这件事

工事中

"很好，"经理说，"可那两个桶里是什么？"

"哦，是这样的，我经过学校会议厅，他们正在召开州教师大会，我就进去卖了一份团体险！"

☆ **urine** /ˈjʊərɪn/ *n.* 尿，小便

☆ **convention** /kənˈvenʃən/ *n.* （正式）会议，（定期）大会

☆ **policy** /ˈpɒləsɪ/ *n.* 保险契约，保险单

How to Annoy Your Co-workers

1. Leave the copy machine set to reduce 200%, extra dark, 17-inch paper, 99 copies.

2. Insist on keeping your car windshield wipers running in all weather conditions "to keep them tuned up."

3. Reply to everything someone says with "that's what YOU think."

4. Finish all your sentences with the words "in accordance with prophecy."

5. Signal that a conversation is over by clamping your hands over your ears.

6. Staple papers in the middle of the page.

7. Ask your co-workers what gender they are.

怎样惹怒同事

1. 将复印机设置为缩印一半的大小，加黑，A3 纸，复印 99 份。

2. 在任何天气状况下都开着前风挡雨刷，好让它随时"在调试中"。

3. 对别人说的事都报以"这只是你的想法"的回答。

4. 用"根据预言所说"来结束你所有的发言。

5. 用双手使劲捂住耳朵来暗示谈话该结束了。

6. 把纸张从中间装订起来。

7. 问同事们他们的性别。

8. While making presentations, occasionally bob your head like a parakeet.

9. Practice making fax and modem noises.

10. During meetings, disassemble your pen and "accidentaly" flip the cartridge across the room.

11. ALWAYS TYPE WITH CAPS-LOCK ON

12. type only in lower case

13. don'tuseanypunctuationorspaceseither

14. Ask your co-workers mysterious questions and then scribble their answers in a notebook.

15. Mutter something about "psychological profiles."

8. 做陈述的过程中，不时地像鹦鹉一样点点头。

9. 练习发出传真机和"猫"的声音。

10. 开会时，拆开你的笔，"不小心"把笔芯弹出来。

11. 全部用大写字母打出

12. 全部用小写字母打出

13. 不要使用标点符号或空格

14. 问同事们诡秘的问题，然后把他们的回答记在小本子上。

15. 嘟嘟嚷嚷一些诸如"心理侧面图"之类的东西。

☆ **windshield** /ˈwɪndʃiːld/ *n.* （汽车前部的）挡风玻璃

☆ **in accordance with** 与…一致；依照，根据

☆ **prophecy** /ˈprɒfɪsɪ/ *n.* 预言；【宗】预言书

☆ **clamp** /klæmp/ *v.* 夹紧；固定

☆ **parakeet** /ˈpærəkiːt/ *n.* 【鸟】长尾小鹦鹉

☆ **disassemble** /ˌdɪsəˈsembl/ *v.* 拆卸，拆开

☆ **scribble** /ˈskrɪbl/ *v.* 潦草书写；涂写

Sleeping Like a Baby

While the stock market was at an all time high, the ups and downs frightened a lot of small investors.

A guy went to his financial adviser and asked if he were worried.

He replied that he slept like a baby.

He was amazed and asked, "Really? Even with all the fluctuations?"

He said, "Yes, that's right. Just like a baby ... I sleep for a couple of hours, then wake up and cry for a couple of hours!"

睡得像个婴儿

股市到了历史高点，散户投资者对这些大起大落心悸不已。

一个人去找他的投资顾问问他是否担心。

顾问回答说他睡得像婴儿一般。

那人吃惊地问："真的吗？在股市有这样大震荡的时候吗？"

顾问说："是的，没错，我睡得像婴儿一般——睡几个小时，然后醒来哭几个小时！"

☆ **fluctuation** /ˌflʌktjʊ'eɪʃən/ *n.* 波动，涨落，起伏

First Name Is OK

The boss of a large company noticed a new employee one day and told him to come into his office.

"What is your name?" was the first thing the boss asked the new guy.

"John," the new guy replied.

The boss scowled, "Look, I don't mind what kind of a place you worked at before, but I don't call anyone by their first name! It breeds familiarity and that leads to a breakdown in authority.

"I refer to my employees by their last name only — Smith, James, Henry — that's all.

名字也好啦

一天，一家大公司的老板注意到一个新来的雇员，于是把他叫到办公室来。

"你叫什么名字？"老板先问道。

"约翰，"新来的答道。

老板皱着眉头说："听着，我不管你以前在什么样的地方工作，可是我们这不会用名字称呼一个人！那样叫法是会有亲切感，但是会导致权威的丧失。"

"我只以姓氏来称呼我的员工——史密斯、詹姆斯、亨利——就是这样，没什么可说的。"

"I am to be referred to only as Mr. Hilton.

"Now that we got that straight，what is your last name?"

The new guy sighed and said，"Darling. My name is John Darling."

"Okay，John，the next thing I want to tell you is. . . ."

118

"你要称呼我为希尔顿先生。"

"现在告诉我你的姓氏是什么？"

新来的叹了一口气说："我姓达林。我叫约翰·达林。"

"好吧，约翰，下面我要说的是……"

☆ scowl /skaʊl/ v. 皱眉；作怒容

☆ breed /briːd/ v. 养育；酿成；产生

☆ get straight 彻底了解，弄清，搞懂

☆ darling /'dɑːlɪŋ/ n. [用作表示亲爱的称呼] 亲爱的

Reasons to Stay at Work All Night

1. Act out your version of a company takeover.

2. Find a way to change everyone's password to "chrysanthemum."

3. Around 2 a.m., play connect-the-dots with lights still on in other office buildings. Keep going until you see a small woodland creature.

4. Sneaking in the boss's desk could land you an unexpected promotion.

5. Draw stick people in all the landscape pictures on the walls, and in the morning, be the first to point out "what a terrible thing that someone did this to such beautiful works of art."

整晚加班的理由

1. 上演一出你接管公司的大戏。

2. 想办法把每个同事的电脑密码改成"chrysanthemum"。

3. 凌晨两点的时候，利用附近大楼里还亮着的灯光玩儿连线游戏，一直到连出一个林地生物。

4. 偷偷翻老板的书桌会让你得到意想不到的提升。

5. 在墙上的风景画上画火柴小人，第二天早上再第一个指出"谁这么讨厌破坏这么美的工艺品"。

6. Go into the other gender's bathroom without fear of being caught.

7. Run up and down the hallways screaming, hoping security will come so you can have someone to talk to.

8. Leave prank messages on the manager's mail.

9. Finally, a chance to live out a dream and pretend to be your boss.

10. Elevator surfing!

6. 不用担惊受怕地进入异性的洗手间。

7. 在大堂里大叫着跑来跑去，希望能把保安招来，好跟他说说话。

8. 在经理的邮箱里留下恶作剧的信息。

9. 终于有了实现梦想的机会，假装是自己的老板。

10. 电梯冲浪！

☆ **chrysanthemum** /krɪˈsænθəməm/ *n.*【植】菊花

☆ **sneak** /sniːk/ *v.* 偷偷地走，潜行

☆ **prank** /præŋk/ *n.* 胡闹，恶作剧

Prepare Three Envelopes

A bright young man had just been hired as the new general manager of a large firm. The manager who was stepping down met with him privately and handed him three numbered envelopes.

"Open one if you encounter a crisis you don't think you can solve," he said.

Well, things went along pretty smoothly, but six months later, everything went wrong. Sales took a nosedive and he was really catching a lot of heat from the board.

At his wit's end, he remembered the three envelopes in his drawer. He hurried back to his office and took out the first envelope.

准备三个信封

一个精明的年轻人刚被任命为一家大公司的总经理。前任经理私下里见了他并给了他三个编了号的信封。

"当你遇到自己无法化解的危机时就打开一个信封，"前任经理说。

刚开始一切进展顺利，可是六个月后，所有事情都变糟了。因为销售额骤降，新任的总经理备受董事会的指责。

全然束手无策之时，他想起了放在抽屉里的三个信封。他赶紧回到办公室，拿出第一个信封。

The message inside read, "Blame your predecessor."

The new manager called a press conference and tactfully laid the blame at the feet of the previous general manager. Satisfied with his comments, the board, the press, and Wall Street responded positively, sales picked up, stock prices rose and the problem was soon behind him.

About a year later, the firm was again experiencing a slight dip in sales, combined with serious product problems. Having learned from his previous experience, the manager wasted no time in opening the second envelope.

The message read, "Reorganize."

里面的纸上写着："抨击你的前任。"

新任总经理召开了一个新闻发布会，圆通得体地把责任推到了前任总经理的身上。董事会满意他的解释，媒体和华尔街也对他的说辞做出了正面的反应，销售额上涨，股票也回升了，问题很快就得到了解决。

又过了一年左右，公司的销售额又出现了小幅下降，还有严重的产品质量问题。有了上次的经验，总经理马上就拆开了第二个信封。

里面的纸上写着："重组。"

This he did, and again the company quickly rebounded.

After several consecutive profitable quarters, the company once again fell on difficult times. The manager went to his office, closed the door and opened the third envelope.

The simple message said, "Prepare three envelopes!"

上班这件事

128

他这样做了，公司很快就重振声威了。

在连续几个季度赢利后，公司再次陷入危机。总经理回到办公室，锁上门，打开了第三个信封。

里面的纸上写着简单的几个字："准备三个信封！"

☆ **step down** 辞职，让位，下台

☆ **encounter**/ɪnˈkaʊntə(r)/ *v.* 意外地遇见；遭到

☆ **nosedive**/ˈnəʊzdaɪv/ *n.* （价格等的）猛跌，暴落

☆ **at sb.'s wit's end** 智穷计尽；全然不知所措

☆ **predecessor**/ˈpriːdɪsesə(r)/ *n.* 前任；前辈

☆ **rebound**/rɪˈbaʊnd/ *v.* 弹回；重新跃起，回升

☆ **consecutive**/kənˈsekjʊtɪv/ *a.* 连续的；连贯的

The Laziest

A site foreman had eight very lazy men working for him, so one day he decided to trick them into doing some work for a change.

"I've got a really easy job today for the laziest one among you," he announced. "Will the laziest man please put his hand up."

Seven hands went up.

"Why didn't you put your hand up?" he asked the eighth man.

"Too much trouble," came the reply.

最懒的

一个工头手下有八个非常懒的工人，终于有一天他想要改变一下现状，于是决定骗他们干活。

"我有一件非常轻松的活要派给你们当中最懒的那个，"他宣布说，"最懒的人举手。"

七只手举了起来。

"你为什么不举手？"他问那第八个人。

"太麻烦了，"那人答道。

☆ trick /trɪk/ v. 哄骗；愚弄

Logical

In a restroom at IBM's Watson Center, a supervisor had placed a sign directly above the sink. It had a single word on it — "THINK!"

The next day, when he went to the restroom, he looked at the sign and right below, immediately above the soap dispenser, someone had carefully lettered another sign which read — "THOAP!"

逻　辑

　　IBM 的一个督察在沃森中心的洗手间的水池上方挂了一块牌子，上面写着："THINK！（思考）"

　　第二天，他去洗手间时，发现在自己放的牌子下方，洗手液盒的上面也有人放了一块牌子，上面写着："THOAP！"

☆ **sink** /sɪŋk/ *n.* 水池

☆ **soap** /səup/ *n.* 肥皂

☆ **dispenser** /dɪsˈpensə(r)/ *n.* 自动售货机；分配器

Is Mr. Smith There

A law firm receptionist answered the phone the morning after the firm's senior partner, Mr. Smith, had passed away unexpectedly.

"Is Mr. Smith there?" asked the client on the phone.

"I'm very sorry, but Mr. Smith passed away last night," the receptionist answered.

"Is Mr. Smith there?" repeated the client.

The receptionist was perplexed. "Perhaps you didn't understand me I'm afraid Mr. Smith passed away last night."

史密斯先生在吗

一家律师事务所的高级合伙人史密斯先生突然去世了。第二天早上接待员接了一个电话。

"史密斯先生在吗?"打电话的客户问。

"很遗憾,史密斯先生昨晚去世了,"接待员答道。

"史密斯先生在吗?"那人又问道。

接待员很困惑:"也许您没听明白,我是说史密斯先生昨晚去世了。"

"Is Mr. Smith there?", asked the client again.

"Sir, do you understand what I'm saying?" said the exasperated receptionist. "Mr. Smith is DEAD!"

"I understand you perfectly," the client sighed. "I just can't hear it often enough."

上班这件事

"史密斯先生在吗?"那人继续问道。

"先生，你明白我在说什么吗?"恼怒的接待员说道，"史密斯先生死了!"

"我太明白你的意思了，"那人叹口气道，"我就是听不够。"

☆ **perplexed** /pə'plekst/ *a.* 困惑的，茫然的

☆ **exasperated** /ɪg'zæspəreitiɪd/ *a.* 被激怒的；恼怒的

I'm Only Kidding

Reaching the end of a job interview, the Human Resources Person asked a young engineer fresh out of MIT, "What starting salary were you looking for?"

The engineer replied, "In the neighborhood of $150,000 a year, depending on the benefits package."

The interviewer said, "Well, what would you say to a package of 5 weeks vacation, 14 paid holidays, full medical and dental, company matching retirement fund to 50% of salary, and a company car leased every 2 years?"

上班这件事

我只是在开玩笑

　　一个刚从麻省理工学院毕业的年轻的工程师去一家公司应聘，面试进行到了最后，人力资源部的面试人员问他："你期望的起薪是多少？"

　　他说："年薪 15 万左右吧，还要看公司的其他福利政策。"

　　面试官说："那么，五周休假，两周带薪年假，医药费全包，退休金基金由公司出一半，每两年租借一辆公司的车给你，你觉得这些福利政策怎么样？"

The young man sat up straight and said, "Wow! Are you kidding?"

The interviewer replied, "Well, yeah, but you started it."

工事中

年轻人坐直了身子，说："天哪！你不是在开玩笑吧?"

面试官答道："我是在开玩笑，不过，这个玩笑是你起的头！"

☆ MIT（Massachusetts Institute of Technology）（美国）麻省理工学院

☆ in the neighborhood of 在…左右，大约

How to Break Down the Cost

The president of a large corporation decided that it was time to build a new factory. He asked representatives from three development companies to come in and make a bid on the project.

The three companies showed up at the scheduled meeting. The president of the large corporation asked the first company whose president earned his MBA from UCLA, "How much will your company charge for this project?"

"20 million, 10 million for materials and 10 million for labor."

The president then asks the same question to the second company whose president earned his MBA from Stanford.

费用怎样分配

　　一家大公司的总裁决定要盖一间新厂房。他约来了三家房产公司的业务代表对这项工程进行竞标。

　　三家公司在约定的时间都到齐了。大公司的总裁问第一家公司："这项工程你们的报价是多少?"这家公司的老板是加利福尼亚大学落杉矶分校的 MBA。

　　"两千万，一千万购买建材，一千万付劳务费。"

　　大公司的总裁又问了第二家公司相同的问题，他们的老板是斯坦福大学的 MBA。

"30 million, 15 million for materials, 13 million for labor, and 2 million for licenses and permits."

Finally, the president asks the last company whose president earned his MBA from USC.

"40 million."

"FOURTY MILLION," yelled the president of the large corporation. "How do you break down the cost?"

"10 million for you, 10 million for me, and 20 million to get the guy from UCLA to build the factory!"

"三千万，一千五百万购买建材，一千三百万付劳务费，两百万用来办理各种许可证。"

最后，大公司的总裁问第三家公司，他们的老板是南加利福尼亚大学的 MBA。

"四千万。"

"四千万！"总裁叫道，"你们怎样用这些钱呢？"

"一千万给你，一千万给我，剩下的两千万把工程包给第一家公司！"

☆ **MBA（Master of Business Administration）**工商管理学硕士

☆ **UCLA（University of California at Los Angeles）**（美国）加利福尼亚大学落杉矶分校

☆ **USC（University of Southern California）**（美国）南加利福尼亚大学

Human Resource Lingo

COMPETITIVE SALARY —

We remain competitive by paying less than our competitors.

JOIN OUR FAST-PACED COMPANY —

We have no time to train you.

CASUAL WORK ATMOSPHERE —

We don't pay enough to expect that you'll dress up.

MUST BE DEADLINE-ORIENTED —

You'll be three months behind schedule on your first day.

SOME OVERTIME REQUIRED —

Some time each night and some time each weekend.

人力资源行话

有竞争力的工资——

我们提供比竞争对手低的工资，这样我们将保持自己的竞争力。

加入我们快速发展的公司——

我们没时间培训你。

宽松的工作环境——

我们付的工资不足以让你盛装打扮。

一定要能按期完成工作——

你来的第一天就已经晚于计划三个月了。

适应不定期加班——

每晚不定期和每个周末不定期。

DUTIES WILL VARY —

Anyone in the office can boss you around.

MUST HAVE AN EYE FOR DETAIL —

We have no quality control.

CAREER-MINDED —

Female Applicants must be childless（and remain that way）.

APPLY IN PERSON —

If you're old，fat or ugly you'll be told the position has been filled.

SEEKING CANDIDATES WITH A WIDE VARIETY OF EXPERIENCE —

You'll need it to replace three people who just left.

适应工作多样——

公司里随便谁都能把你支使来支使去。

一定要注意细节——

我们没有质量监控系统。

有事业心——

女性求职者不能有孩子（而且要把这种状态一直保持下去）。

要求本人亲自来求职——

如果你岁数太大，或是太胖，或是太难看，我们就会告诉你这个职位已经没有空缺了。

寻求有多种工作经历的人——

你要填补刚离开的三个人的空缺。

PROBLEM-SOLVING SKILLS A MUST —

You're walking into a company in perpetual chaos.

REQUIRES TEAM LEADERSHIP SKILLS —

You'll have the responsibilities of a manager, without the pay or respect.

GOOD COMMUNICATION SKILLS —

Management communicates, you listen, figure out what they want and do it.

150

具备解决问题的能力——

你正要步入一家永远杂乱无章的公司。

要求具备团队领导才能——

你将承担经理的职责，但是不会有相应的报酬，也得不到相应的尊重。

良好的沟通技能——

管理层传达意见，你听后想法弄明白然后执行。

☆ **lingo** /ˈlɪŋgəʊ/ *n.* 行话，术语

☆ **perpetual** /pəˈpetjʊəl/ *a.* 永久的；无休止的

☆ **chaos** /ˈkeɪɒs/ *n.* 混乱，紊乱

A Day off

So you want a day off. Let's take a look at what you are asking for.

There are 365 days per year available for work.

There are 52 weeks per year in which you already have 2 days off per week, leaving 261 days available for work.

Since you spend 16 hours each day away from work, you have used up 170 days, leaving only 91 days available.

You spend 30 minutes each day on coffee break. That counts for 23 days each year, leaving only 68 days available.

请一天假

你想要请一天假，让我们来看看你在要求什么。

一年有 365 天。

一年有 52 个星期，每个星期有两个休息日，这样一年就剩下 261 个工作日了。

一天中你有 16 小时是不工作的，这样又占去了 170 天，就只剩下 91 个工作日了。

每天你还有 30 分钟的工间休，这样又占用了 23 天，就只剩下 68 个工作日了。

With a 1 hour lunch each day, you used up another 46 days, leaving only 22 days available for work.

You normally spend 2 days per year on sick leave. This leaves you only 20 days per year available for work.

We are off 5 holidays per year, so your available working time is down to 15 days.

We generously give 14 days vacation per year which leaves only 1 day available for work and I'll be damned if you are going to take that day off!!!

上
班
这
件
事

每天你还要花一小时吃午饭，这样又用掉了 46 天，就只剩下 22 个工作日了。

一年里你通常还会休两天的病假，这样就剩下 20 个工作日了。

我们还有 5 天的年假，这样工作日就只有 15 天了。

我们还慷慨地给了你两周的休假时间，这样你就只有一天工作了，我绝对不会让你在那一天请假的！！！

☆ **I'll be damned if . . .** 我决不…，我绝对不…

What Is Three Times Three?

Three elderly ladies were at the doctor for a cognitive reasoning test.

The doctor says to the first lady, "What is three times three?"

"297," was her prompt reply.

"Ummm humm," the doctor shook his head.

The doctor says to the second lady, "It's your turn now. What is three times three?"

"Sunday," replies the second lady.

"Ummm humm . . ."

Then the doc says to the third, "Okay, Madam, your turn. What's three times three?"

3 乘以 3 得多少？

三个老太太在医生那里做认知推理测试。

医生问第一个老太太："3 乘以 3 得多少？"

"297，"她答道。

"啊——啊——"医生摇摇头。

医生接着问第二个老太太，"轮到你了，3 乘以 3 得多少？"

"星期天，"她答道。

"啊——啊——"

医生再问第三个老太太，"现在，夫人，该你了，3 乘以 3 得多少？"

"Nine," she says.

"That's wonderful!" says the doctor. "Tell me, how did you get that?"

"Simple," she says, "I subtracted 297 from Sunday!"

"9，"她说。

"太棒了！"医生说，"告诉我，你是怎么算出来的？"

"很简单，"她说，"用星期天减去 297！"

☆ **cognitive** /ˈkɒgnɪtɪv/ *a.* 认识的，认识能力的

☆ **subtract** /səbˈtrækt/ *v.* 减，减去

A Big Glass of Water

A man goes to the doctor and tells him that he hasn't been feeling well. The doctor examines him, leaves the room and comes back with three different bottles of pills.

The doctor says, "Take the green pill with a big glass of water when you get up. Take the blue pill with a big glass of water after lunch. Then just before going to bed, take the red pill with another big glass of water."

Startled to be put on so much medicine the man stammers, "By Jesus, exactly what's my problem?"

Doctor says, "You're not drinking enough water."

160

一大杯水

一个人去看医生，说自己身体不适。医生为他做了检查后走出了诊室，回来的时候手里拿了三瓶药。

医生说："你起床的时候用一大杯水送服绿色的药片。吃完午饭后用一大杯水送服蓝色的药片。睡觉前再用一大杯水送服红色的药片。"

要吃这么多药把那人吓住了，他结结巴巴地问："天哪，我到底得了什么病？"

医生说："你喝水喝得不够。"

☆ **stammer** /ˈstæmə(r)/ *v.* 结结巴巴地说，口吃

Never Got Caught

A man was filling out a job application.

When he came to the question, "Have you ever been arrested?" he wrote, "No."

The next question, intended for people who had answered in the affirmative to the previous question, was "Why?"

The man answered it anyway, "Never got caught!"

从没被抓住过

一个人在填写一份求职申请。

对于"你是否被逮捕过？"这个问题，他填上了"否"的回答。

下一个问题是针对那些填写了"是"的人而问的——"为什么？"

那人也填写了回答："从没被抓住过！"

You're Finished

Manager (to the applicant): We are very keen on cleanliness. Did you wipe your feet on the mat as you came in?

Applicant: Yes, sir.

Manager: We are also keen on truthfulness. There is no mat there at all.

上班这件事

164

你完了

经理（对应聘者）：我们非常注重清洁。你进来的时候有没有在门垫上蹭蹭脚啊？

应聘者：有的，先生。

经理：我们同样非常注重诚实的品德。那里根本就没有门垫。

☆ **truthfulness** /ˈtruːθfʊlnɪs/ *n.* 诚实，讲真话

Sick Leave Policy

TO ALL EMPLOYEES

SICKNESS

No excuse ... We will no longer accept your doctor's statement as proof. We believe that if you are able to go to the doctor, you are able to come to work.

AN OPERATION

We are no longer allowing this practice. We wish to discourage any thoughts that you may need an operation. We believe that as long as you are an employee here, you will need all of whatever you have and should not consider having anything removed. We hired you as you

病假政策

致全体员工

生病

生病不是不来上班的理由。我们将不再取信医生的诊断证明。我们认为如果你能去医院看病，就能来上班。

手术

我们不再允许员工去做手术。我们希望打消任何你可能需要做手术的念头。我们认为只要你还是这里的员工，就应该保证自己的完整性，而不应该考虑动手术切除任何部分。我们雇用的是完整的你，如果你切除了某个部位，就肯定与我们的预期有差距了。

are, and to have anything removed would certainly make you less than we bargained for.

DEATH

Other Than Your Own

This is no excuse for missing work. There is nothing you can do for them, and we are sure that someone else can attend to the arrangements. However, if the funeral can be held in the late afternoon, we will be glad to allow you to work through your lunch hour and subsequently let you leave 1 hour early, provided your share of the work is ahead enough to keep the job going in your absence.

Your Own

This will be accepted as an excuse. However, we require at least two weeks notice

上班这件事

工事中

死亡

除非是你死了

否则这不能成为不来上班的理由。你不能为死去的人做什么，而且我们确信还有别人会为葬礼做准备工作。当然，如果葬礼在傍晚时分举行，我们将很乐意允许你利用午饭时间工作，然后提前一小时下班。前提是你的那份工作能够提前做好，这样你不在时，其他的工作不会受到影响。

你死了

这是我们能够接受的不来上班的理由。但是，要提前两个星期通知，因为培训你的继任者是你的职责。

as we feel it is your duty to train your replacement.

ALSO

Entirely too much time is being spent in the restroom. In the future, we will follow the practice of going in alphabetical order. For instance, those whose names begin with "A" will go from 8:00 - 8:15, and so on. If you're unable to go at your time, it will be necessary to wait until the next day when your time comes again.

We appreciate your cooperation.

THE MANAGEMENT

另外

员工在洗手间里浪费的时间太多。今后，我们将执行按字母顺序分时段使用洗手间的政策。比如，姓名以"A"开头的员工将在 8 点到 8 点 15 分使用洗手间，以此类推。如果在规定的时间没能够去成，就只能等到第二天。

感谢你们的合作。

管理层

Boss Quotes

We are going to continue having these meetings, everyday, until I find out why no work is getting done.

I didn't say it was your fault. I said I was going to blame it on you.

The beatings will continue until morale improves.

We passed over a lot of good people to get the ones we hired.

I'm sorry if I ever gave you the impression your input would have any effect on my decision for the outcome of this project!

老板的话

这样的会议我们要每天开，一直开下去，直到我弄清楚为什么工作没有完成。

我没说这是你的错，我只是说要归咎于你。

精神面貌改变了才能扭转败局。

为了找到我们要用的人，我们刷掉了很多人才。

如果我给了你你会影响到我对这个项目的决策这种印象的话，我很抱歉！

上班这件事

What you see as a glass ceiling, I see as a protective barrier.

I see you've had no computer training. Although that qualifies you for upper management, it means you're under-qualified for our entry level positions.

你眼里的玻璃天花板是我的保护墙。

我注意到你没有接受过电脑知识的相关培训，虽然这一点使你有资格进入管理层，但是你却不能胜任我们的初级职位。

I'm the Boss

The boss was complaining in our staff meeting the other day that he wasn't getting any respect.

Later that morning he went to a local card and novelty shop and bought a small sign that read, "I'm the Boss."

He then taped it to his office door.

Later that day when he returned from lunch, he found that someone had taped a note to the sign that said, "Your wife called, she wants her sign back!"

我是老板

一天，老板在员工大会上抱怨说他没有得到应得的尊重。

当天上午他就去卡片饰品店买了一个小标牌，上面写着："我是老板"。

然后把它粘在了他办公室的门上。

到了中午，他吃完午饭回来，看到有人在标牌上粘了一张纸条，上面写着："你妻子打电话来，她想要回她的标牌！"

Job Interview No-No's!

If you really want that new job, you may want to avoid saying these:

I'm really keen to work for you, I hear the drugs are good.

I regret that I have no references. Unfortunately, every company I have worked for has since closed down.

I'll kill myself if I don't get a job.

I know where you live.

I'm really tall, so I think I'd be well suited to this job.

By the way, I understand that you have an unmarried daughter.

I won't sue you when you fire me.

上班这件事

工事中

178

应聘面试时千万不要说！

如果你真想得到那份新工作，就不要说下面这些话：

我非常想为你们工作，听说那些麻醉剂很不错。

很遗憾我没有一个推荐人。不幸的是，我工作过的每家公司都在录用我后倒闭了。

找不到工作我会杀了我自己的。

我知道你住在哪儿。

我的个子真的很高，所以我认为自己很胜任这份工作。

顺便提一句，我知道你还有个未婚的女儿。

你们解雇我时我不会告你们。

I'll work so hard you won't even know I'm there.

You can't turn me down because I smell bad. You have to have a reason.

If you call the people I listed as references，please call my parole officer last.

That big thing growing on my face isn't my fault.

If you hired my dumb-ass brother then you can surely hire me.

My arrest record is all a bunch of lies.

I was a sniper in the Army.

The only reason my grades in High School was so bad was because all the teachers thought I was stupid because I didn't pass the tests. They weren't being fair to me because they don't like me.

上班这件事

我会卖力工作，你都不会注意到我。

你们不能因为我口臭就不要我，你们要给我个理由。

如果你们要给我的推荐人们打电话，请最后打给我的假释官。

我脸上长这大家伙不是我的错。

如果你们能录用我那蠢哥哥，就一定能录用我。

我的入狱记录完全是一派胡言。

我在部队时是狙击手。

我在高中成绩那么烂是因为我的老师们因为我考试不及格而认为我笨。他们不喜欢我，所以对我不公正。

If you hire me you can blow your nose on my sleeve any time you want to.

If you hire me don't tell the Welfare until I get my Jeep paid off.

If you hire me I will show up. That's all I can promise for sure, but maybe it will be better than that and I will sure try.

When do we eat?

How long do I have to work here before I can collect unemployment again?

I won't have to do anything, will I?

Can I bring my goat to the company daycare center?

I collect guns. You probably want to tell me that I got the job now, right?

如果你录用我，就可以随时在我的袖子上擤鼻子。

如果你们录用了我，请在我付清大吉普的钱后再把我被录用的消息告诉福利救济署。

如果你们录用了我，我一定会来上班。这是我保证能做到的，当然也许会更好，我会努力的。

我们什么时候吃饭？

在我下次能领救济金前，我得在这工作多长时间？

我不用做任何事，是吧？

我能把我的山羊放在公司的日托中心吗？

我收集枪支。你可能想对我说我得到这份工作了，是吧？

☆ **parole** /pəˈrəʊl/ *n.* 假释

☆ **sniper** /ˈsnaɪpə(r)/ *n.* 狙击手

外文出版社精品阅读图书推荐

21世纪英语沙龙丛书（英汉对照）

生活小品文	西方风情录	名言荟萃
妙语拾趣	笑话集锦	寓言世界
名人掠影	名人轶事	

心灵阅读（英汉对照）

人生篇　励志篇　情感篇　生活篇
情操篇　道德篇　箴言篇

西方风情系列读本（英汉对照）

礼仪与风俗　节日与婚礼　饮食与生活
时尚与休闲

笑话集锦（英汉对照）

婚姻悟语　校园逸事　男人与女人
上班这件事　童言无忌　动物趣闻
钱这东西

品读人生丛书（英汉对照）

关于爱：有爱走过
关于幸福：幸福的滋味
关于理想：梦开始的地方
关于成功：生命的辉煌
关于自信：相信你自己
关于处世：美丽心世界